PUPIL'S BOOK 5

Welcome 2

1 Adventure camp 4

Wider World 1 12

2 Wildlife park 14

3 Where I live 22

Wider World 2 30

4 Good days 32

5 Trips 40

Wider World 3 48

6 Arts 50

7 Space 58

Wider World 4 66

8 Environment 68

Goodbye 76

Grammar round-up 78

Festival 80

Welcome

Adventure camp

1 What camping words do you know? Can you say them?

2 1:05 Listen and read. Who is Tom's sister?

Adventure Camp!

Remember to bring these things:

tent   sleeping bag
pegs   compass
rucksack   torch

Please send in information about yourself by 20th May.
See you there!

Hannah: Hi, there. I'm Hannah. What are your names?
Maria: I'm Maria.
Felipe: And I'm Felipe.
Tom: I'm Tom and this is my sister...
Flo: I'm Flo.
Hannah: Great, let's see... Maria... Felipe... Tom... Flo... Welcome to the camp, guys!

3 1:06 Listen and say.

1
sleeping bag

2
tent

3
poles

6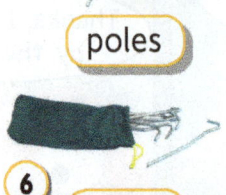
pegs

4
first-aid kit

5
rucksack

7
torch

8
compass

4   Play the game.

A: I went camping and in my tent there was a sleeping bag.
B: I went camping and in my tent there was a sleeping bag and a...

Can identify camping equipment

5 **Read and answer.** *True* **or** *false*?

My name is Tom. I'm fourteen and I'm British. I love playing basketball and football. I can cook and swim but I can't surf. I've got one sister, Flo. She's twelve and she's very funny.

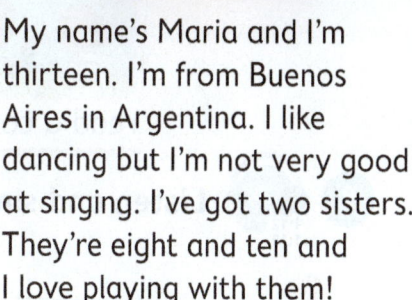

My name's Maria and I'm thirteen. I'm from Buenos Aires in Argentina. I like dancing but I'm not very good at singing. I've got two sisters. They're eight and ten and I love playing with them!

I'm Flo and I'm twelve. I'm from Britain. I'm good at swimming and I love talking to my friends. I've got one brother. He's fourteen and he's very good at sports. He's very clever, too.

1 Tom can swim and surf.
2 Flo is good at swimming.
3 Flo loves talking to friends.
4 Maria's British.
5 Felipe's got two brothers.

I'm Felipe. I'm from Valencia in Spain. I'm thirteen. I love playing computer games and I like Science and Maths. I've got three brothers and they love computer games, too. We always have competitions!

1:08

I **love** play**ing** basketball.
I**'m good at** swim**ming**.

6 **Read the questions and write answers in your notebook. Ask and answer.**

1 Where are Tom and Flo from?
2 What does Tom love doing?
3 How old are Maria's sisters?
4 What subjects does Felipe like?

7 **Choose someone from Activity 5. Ask and answer.**

1 How old are you?
2 Where are you from?
3 What do you like doing?
4 What are you good at?
5 Have you got any brothers or sisters?

8 **Listen and say.**

1
pitch a tent

2
keep out the rain

3
put in the pegs

4
read a compass

5
lay out the bed

6
cover our heads

9 **Listen and sing. How many activities can you find?**

Scouts from all around the world, from Spain to Italy.
We're travelling together, from the mountains to the sea.
We walk for miles and learn every day.
We read a compass and find our way.

Chorus:
Oh, we are adventure scouts, here is our song.
With adventure and new friends, you can't go wrong.
You can't go wrong.

At the end of the day, we're back to camp again.
We're pitching our tents, they keep out the rain.
We're putting in the pegs and laying out our beds.
We're sleeping in sleeping bags that cover our heads!

Chorus

All this adventure is making us fit and strong.
We're cooking our food which doesn't take too long.
We're eating our dinner and then we're so tired.
We're sleeping in tents all around the fire!

Chorus

10  **Read and say.**

1 He / cook dinner
2 They / sit in a circle
3 I / read a compass
4 She / put in the pegs
5 We / pitch a tent

LOOK!
We**'re reading** a compass.
We**'re putting** in the pegs.

11 **Play the game.**

A: What am I doing?   **B:** You're reading a compass!

Lesson 3   Can identify camping activities

12 **Read. Where was Flo yesterday?**

1st July

Dear Mum,

How are you? It's our fourth day at camp and we're having a great time. We've got some new friends, too – they're from Spain and Argentina. They're teaching me Spanish but I'm not very good at it!

Our first day was great. There was a big dinner to welcome everyone and there were songs by the campfire. Our tent was cold but it was warm in the sleeping bag.

Yesterday, we went for a walk in the forest next to the camp. The trees were very tall and there were a lot of cool animals there. Here's a photo of me with my new friends.

Love to you and Dad,

Flo

13 **Read and choose.**

1 Flo's new friends are from Spain and (Italy / Argentina).

2 Flo is learning (Spanish / Italian).

3 There was a big (lunch / dinner) on their first day.

4 It (was / wasn't) cold in the sleeping bag.

5 They went for a walk in the (forest / city) yesterday.

14   **Ask and answer.**

1 Do you like camping?

2 Where do you go camping?

3 What activities do you do there?

SOUNDS FUN!

15   **Listen, read and say.**

Theo's teaching the trees to
tell the time.
They said, 'Thanks, Theo.
It's three o'clock.'
But it was half past nine!

MATT IS TELLING BELLA ABOUT THEIR TIME JOURNEY.

1

...so these weird guys took our new THD and went off in time!

There! It's working now. What is it anyway?

2

It's a THD, a time hole detector. You can travel through time with it.

Wow! Can we try it?

3

Haven't you got stuff to do here?

Um, not really.

TODAY'S TASKS
PITCH TENTS
READ COMPASSES
LIGHT FIRES
KEEP OUT OF THE RAIN
TAKE DOWN TENTS

4

This looks fun! Don't you like camping?

Yes, I love camping but come on, TIME TRAVEL?

5

Sir! There's a new trace! They're going to – Africa!

Oh, WOW! Please let me come.

She is good at computers, sir. That could be useful.

6

Oh, PLEASE!

Oh, all right.

AL, let's follow those guys.

  Act out the story.

Lesson 5 Can understand a simple story / Can discuss a story

18 **What do you know?**

19 **1:19** Read. What is Bear's job?

Bear Grylls

Bear Grylls is a mountaineer and adventurer. He went up Mount Everest when he was just twenty-three years old! Bear usually lives in the United Kingdom but sometimes he lives in the desert, the mountains or the jungle. He is also Chief Scout of Scouts UK.

1 What do you like doing?
I like playing the guitar, running, doing yoga and playing with my children.

2 Do you like living in the jungle?
I love jungles but they're difficult to live in. There are often a lot of snakes and insects. Sometimes I sleep up in a tree and when it rains, it's horrible.

3 Where is your favourite place?
An island in Indonesia. I love visiting islands and this one was really beautiful.

4 What do you do before an adventure?
I always learn a lot about where I want to go – I learn about the plants and animals. I train six days a week and I run and do yoga, too. I also prepare my survival kit.

5 Are you scared of anything?
Yes, I'm scared of high buildings and mountains but I just stay calm. It isn't easy.

20 Read and say. *True* or *false?*

1 Bear does yoga before a trip.
2 Jungles are difficult to live in.
3 Bear doesn't take a survival kit.

> I'm going to Mount Everest in Nepal.

> I'm taking a big rucksack with lots of things...

MINI PROJECT

21 Prepare for an adventure trip.

- **Ideas** – Imagine you are going to the jungle or mountains.

- **Plan** – Make notes. Where are you going? What do you need to take?

- **Write** – Answer these questions with 1–2 sentences. Where are you going? Why? How can you prepare? What will you take? What are you scared of?

- **Share** – Interview a classmate about their adventure.

HOME SCHOOL LINK

22 **Match.**

1 You do this to find your way.

2 You put these in when pitching the tent.

3 You do this before going to sleep.

4 You do this when it rains.

5 You are warm when you use this.

a sleeping bag

b read a compass

c pegs

d lay out the bed

e cover your head

23  **Listen and tick (✓) or cross (✗).**

1:20

		likes	loves	is good at
1	Sally	a ▢	b ▢	c ▢
2	Pete	a ▢	b ▢	c ▢

24 **Find and write questions. Then look at Activity 23 and write answers.**

1 Sally / doing / love / does / what

_____

2 Sally / what / at / good / is

_____

3 Pete / a / is / compass / at / reading / good

_____

25  **Ask and answer.**

1 What do you like doing? What do you not like doing?

2 What are you good at? What are you not good at?

3 What do you do when you go camping?

I can identify camping equipment and activities.

I can say what people are/aren't good at doing.

I can say what people like/don't like doing.

I can plan an adventure trip.

26 **Write answers about you. Then guess about your partner.**

What are you good at?
A: _____   B: _____
What are you not good at?
A: _____   B: _____
What do you like doing?
A: _____   B: _____
What don't you like doing?
A: _____   B: _____
What subjects do you like?
A: _____   B: _____
What subjects don't you like?
A: _____   B: _____
What sports do you like?
A: _____   B: _____
What sports don't you like?
A: _____   B: _____

27   **I want to know more!**

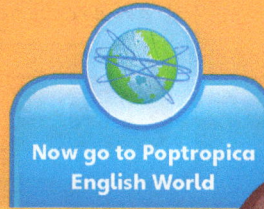
Now go to Poptropica
English World

Wider World 1
Camping around the world

1 ⭐ What do you know?

2 🎧 **1:22** Look and say. Guess the countries. Then listen and check.

3 Read. Match the highlighted words with the photos.

a

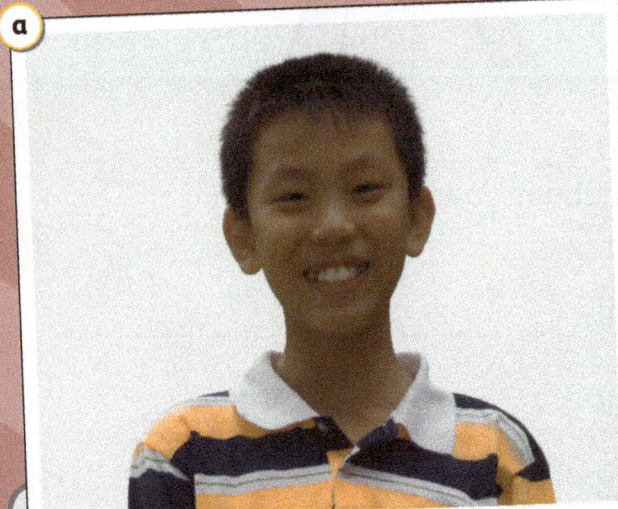

Camping in Thailand is great fun. My favourite place is a national park called Khao Sam Roi Yot. Khao Sam Roi Yot means the mountain with 300 peaks.
The mountains are very difficult to climb. I like watching the lovely birds and other wild animals like deer and squirrels. There are a lot of interesting caves, too. Thailand is an exciting place!

> Alak, 12, Thailand

b

Death Valley National Park in California is a great place for desert camping. I usually visit Death Valley in the spring with my family. I love riding my bike on the paths in the mountains. Mountain biking is difficult but it's very exciting. My dad likes making big campfires in the evening. He likes cooking our dinner on the fire. There are many types of snakes, lizards and birds in Death Valley. It's never boring in the desert!

> Melissa, 12, the USA

Can understand texts about camping around the world

Vulcano is a small volcanic island in Italy. I like camping there in the summer with my grandparents. We sleep in a small cabin in the forest. I like hiking to the top of the volcano. My granny likes walking on the black sandy beaches near the sea. There is special mud in Vulcano that is very good for your skin. Some people like putting the mud on their bodies. I love visiting Vulcano!

Luca, 11, Italy

4 Read again. *True* or *false*?

1 The mountains in Thailand are easy to climb.
2 Alak likes watching birds.
3 Death Valley is in the desert.
4 Melissa doesn't like riding her bike.
5 Vulcano is a big island.
6 Luca likes hiking.

5 Ask and answer.

1 Do you like camping?
2 Where can you camp in your country?

YOUR TURN!

Think of your ideal place to camp. Imagine you go camping there every summer. Describe it.

Where is it?
Who do you go with?
What do you like doing there?

Wildlife park

1  Do you know the names of any wild animals?
What can you say about them?

2  **1:23** Listen and read. Where was Flo?

1

There you all are! Where *were* you?

2

We were with the cheetahs. They were *really* fast!

3

I was with the snakes. They were *really* long!

4

I was with the elephant.

Cool! How big was it?

Really big! *And* it was really naughty!

3  **1:24** Listen and say.

1 rhino

2 cheetah

3 tortoise

4 snake

5 elephant

6 koala

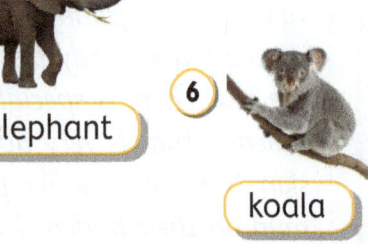

4  Play the game. You have one minute.

A: Slow.　　**B:** Tortoises are slow.

Can identify wild animals

5 🎧 1:26 **Listen, look and say. Which animal is Tom with?**

Name: Roddy
How heavy? 1,600 kilograms
How tall? 2 metres
How long? 3 metres
How fast? fast!

Name: Geri
How heavy? 800 kilograms
How tall? 5 metres
How long? 3 metres
How fast? fast!

6  **Look and make questions. Then ask and answer.**

1 tall / the giraffe?   **2** heavy / the rhino?   **3** fast / the rhino?
4 long / the giraffe?   **5** tall / the rhino?   **6** heavy / the giraffe?

A: How tall is it?
B: It's 5 metres tall.

🎧 1:27 **LOOK!**

| How heavy is it? | It's 800 kilograms. |
| How tall is it? | It's about 5 metres tall. |

7  **Choose an animal. Ask and answer.**

A: How long is it?
B: It's 1.8 metres long.

5,000 kilograms
3.5 metres

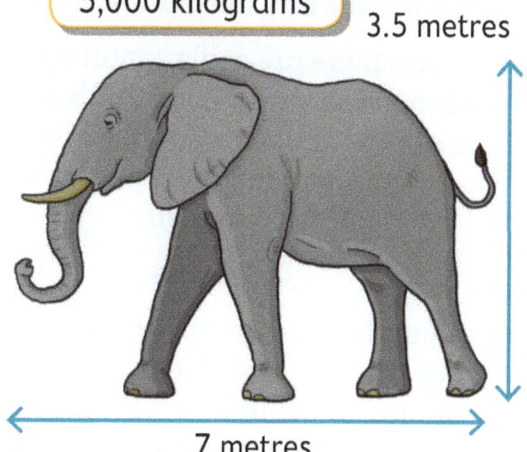

45 kilograms
0.8 metres

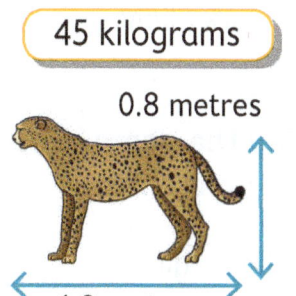

1.8 metres

200 kilograms
1.2 metres

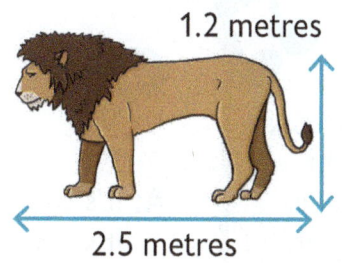

2.5 metres

7 metres

8 🎧 1:29 **Listen and say.**

1 tiger
2 panther
3 lemur
4 emu
5 turtle
6 whale
7 meerkat
8 otter
9 seal

9 🎧 1:31 **Listen and sing. How many animals are in the song?**

Chorus:
Take me to a place where the days are longer,
Where I can be with the animals, wild and free.
Take me to a place where the trees are taller
Than the houses and the buildings in the big city.

In the sea there are seals, smaller than otters.
There are blue whales, longer than my street.
Can you see the turtles, swimming in the blue water?
They're bigger than my pet fish but they've got feet!

Chorus

In the jungle there are tigers, faster than taxis.
There are panthers, darker than the night.
I want to see the lemurs, sitting in the trees.
I really love wild animals, orange, black or white!

10 **Read and say.** *Jungle, sea* or *mountains*?

1	tigers	2	seals
3	lemurs	4	goats
5	whales	6	turtles
7	eagles	8	panthers

Jungle!

🎧 1:32 **LOOK!**

They're **bigger than** my pet fish.

11 **Look and say.**

1 Giraffes / tall / tigers
2 Lemurs / fast / rhinos
3 Elephants / heavy / turtles
4 Koalas / slow / cheetahs
5 Panthers / dark / lions

12 **Play the game. Guess the animal.**

A: It's shorter than a giraffe.
It's faster than a panther.
B: It's a cheetah!

13 **Read. Is Vernie happier now?**

PLEASE SPONSOR VERNIE!

To sponsor Vernie now, click on this link.

Please sponsor me!

Vernie's Story

Jen from the Koala Reserve says. 'Here at the reserve, we've got a lot of rescued koalas. They live longer here and they are happier here than in the wild.

Vernie the koala was in the wild for years. Her home was next to a road. It was very dangerous. Her joey, a baby koala, died one day on the road. Vernie was very sad.

We went to the forest one day, looking for sick koalas. Vernie was next to the road. She was not happy and she was sick.'

Now, she is safe, happy and healthy in our koala reserve. Please sponsor her!

14 **Read again and answer.**

1 Where was Vernie's home?
2 What does 'joey' mean?
3 Was Vernie happier in the wild?
4 Was Vernie healthy in the wild?
5 Where is Vernie now?

15 **Match the places with the animals. Think of three more with a friend.**

> Africa   Asia   Australia

1 cheetahs   2 koalas
3 elephants   4 tigers

SOUNDS FUN!

16 **1:33** **Listen, read and say.**

The cle**v**er, hea**v**y **w**alruses lo**v**e **v**iolins on **W**ednesdays.

Talk about the pictures. Then listen and read.

1 THE THD IS WORKING NOW.

I can't see anyone.

Over there! They're getting away, quick!

2 Rhinos can run at 50 km per hour. But the cheetah is faster than all animals. It can...

Oh, um, quick!

Oh, PLEASE be QUIET!

3 Is the rhino still there?

No. And those guys that took the THD aren't here, either.

Um, how do we get down?

4 It's lucky I had this rope.

Yeah, and you can tie knots!

5 Hello, little guy.

Um, is that a cheetah?

The cheetah is faster than the rhino...

6 QUICK! Get us out of here!

  Act out the story.

19 What do you know?

20  **1:38** Find the chameleons in the photos. Then read.

Cool camouflage for chameleons!

Chameleons are one of the strangest animals in the world. There are 160 kinds of chameleons and many can change colour. Here are some more facts about them.

Size: They are sometimes smaller than your finger. Some are longer than your arm! Females are often smaller than males.

Body: They have got very long tongues and their feet have got claws. They are very good at climbing.

Colour: Chameleons are very clever - they use colour to show how they feel or to hide. They can change colour when they are scared, angry, hot or cold. For example, a panther chameleon turns red when it is angry.

Places: A lot of chameleons live in Madagascar in Africa. Some live in India, too. They like hot, dry places.

Food: Chameleons eat insects and they are good at catching flies with their long tongues. Some big chameleons can eat small birds.

Lifespan: They usually live for five to ten years. They live longer when they are kept as pets than in the wild.

21 Ask and answer.

1 What do chameleons look like?
2 When do they change colour?
3 Where do they live?
4 What do they eat?

MINI PROJECT

22 Find out about an interesting animal.

- **Ideas** – Think about an interesting animal you know.

- **Plan** – Make notes about size/body/colour/places/food/lifespan.

- **Write** – Write 1–2 sentences about each of these things.

- **Share** – Tell a classmate about your animal.

HOME SCHOOL LINK

23 **Read and circle.**

1 The giraffe is five (kilograms / metres) tall.
2 How (heavy / tall / long) is the rhino? It's 1,600 kilograms.
3 Cheetahs are (fast / faster) than lions.
4 Meerkats are (smaller / bigger) than lemurs.

24 1:39 **Listen, tick (✓) and circle.**

1 **a** **b**

bigger / faster

2 **a** **b**

lighter / taller

3 **a** **b**

fast / faster

4 **a** **b**

heavy / heavier

25 **Look at Activity 24 and write.**

1 _____
2 _____
3 _____
4 _____

26  **Look at the photos in Activity 24. Ask and answer about the animals.**

A Are turtles bigger than whales?

B No, they aren't.

I CAN

I can talk about which animal is big/long/slow/fast.
I can compare animals using *bigger/longer/slower/faster than*.
I can find out and talk about an interesting animal.

27 Read the clues. Write the animals' names.

Down ▼

1 It's a large land animal. It has got one or two horns.

2 It looks like a small monkey and has got a long tail.

4 It's a large land animal with a long trunk and big ears.

5 It's an orange cat with black stripes.

9 It's a large animal with flippers. It eats fish and lives in the sea.

12 This animal is the 'king' of the animal world.

13 It's an African animal. It has got black and white stripes.

Across ▶▶▶

3 It's the fastest land animal in the world.

6 It's a very large mammal that lives in the sea.

7 This animal eats fish and is about one metre long.

8 It's in the cat family and is usually black.

10 It's a large sea reptile that has got a thick shell.

11 It's quieter than a chimpanzee but much bigger.

14 It's an Australian animal that looks like a small bear.

28  Look at Unit 1, page 4. Ask and answer more questions with -er words.

Is the first-aid kit lighter than the compass?

29   I want to know more!

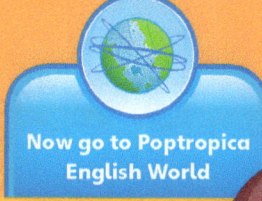
Now go to Poptropica English World

3 Where I live

1 ⭐ What names of places in a town do you know? Can you say them?

2 🎧 1:41 Listen and read. What is Flo doing?

Phew! 450 steps!

I'm hot now! I want to go swimming! Where's the swimming pool?

It's there – near the cinema. But where's Flo?

Oh, no! She's got the money!

Look! She's there – near the park. What's she doing?

She's buying ice cream! I want ice cream, too! Come on!

3 🎧 1:42 Listen and match. Then listen and say.

> castle   cinema   library   park
> shopping centre   supermarket   swimming pool

4  Talk about your town or village.

There's a cinema but there isn't a castle.

Can identify places in a town

5   **Listen. Choose the correct picture.**

1 **a**  **b**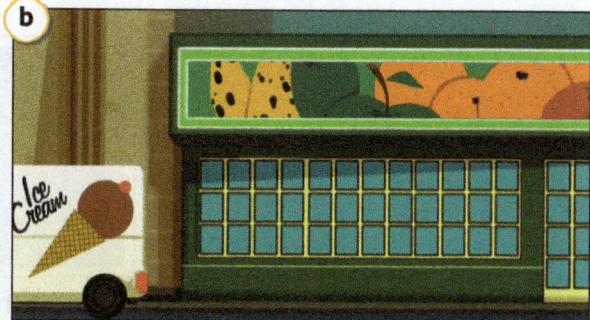

2 **a**  **b**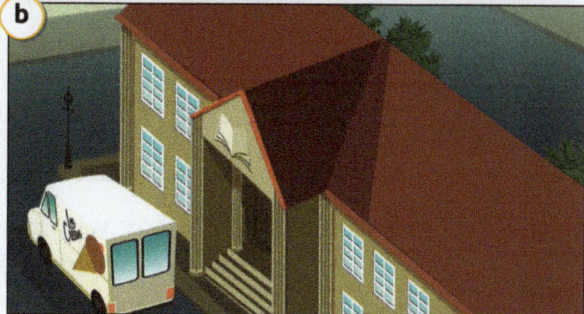

3 **a**  **b**

 **LOOK!**

①	②	③	④	⑤	⑥

next to	opposite	near	in front of	between	behind

6 **Look at the *Look!* box. Where's the mouse?**

A: Where's the mouse in Number 1?
B: The mouse is next to the box.

7 **Look at the town on page 22 again. Play.**

It's opposite the park and next to the cinema. What is it?

It's the...

8 1:46 **Listen and say.**

1	2	3	4	5	6
town	sunset	rain	city	sky	clouds

9 1:47 1:48 **Listen and sing. Does the boy like the city?**

I love sitting by my window.
I love watching the world go by.
I want to stay forever.
I want to watch the sunset in the sky.
Do you want to watch with me? (x2)

I don't like walking in the city,
With people running up and down.
No time for listening, no time for talking.
I don't want to live in this mad town.
Do you want to walk with me? (x2)

I love sitting by my window.
I love watching the clouds up high.
I want to stay forever.
I want to watch the rain fall from the sky.
Do you want to come with me? (x2)

10  **Look and say. Make sentences.**

1 I / not want to / live in a city
2 you / want to / watch the sunset?
3 He / not want to / go to the park
4 she / want to / play basketball?

 1:49 **LOOK!**

I **want to watch** the sun.

I **don't want to waste** my time.

Do you **want to watch** it with me?

11  **Tell a friend. Do you like noisy cities or quiet places? Why?**

I like noisy cities because…

12 **Read. Where does Alex live?**

From: alex@yoohoo.com

To: jack@nmail341.com

Hi Jack,

I'm writing to you because I want to have an e-pal in a big city. I love sending emails to friends.

I live in a village on Sark. Sark is a very small island in Britain, near France. Only 600 people live on Sark. I'm happy here because my family and friends are here. I love school, too. We sometimes play sports but often there aren't many people to play on two teams. The beaches here are very clean but they're very quiet. There aren't any shopping centres on the island. We go by boat for an hour to another island to go to a shopping centre! On Sark, there isn't an airport and there aren't any cars. We ride our bikes everywhere.

I want to make new friends from different places. Do you like living in Liverpool? Is it a big city? Please email or phone me soon.

Alex

13 **Read the sentences. *True* or *false*?**

1 Alex likes emailing his friends.
2 Sark is a big island.
3 Alex doesn't like Sark.
4 There is a shopping centre on Sark.
5 You can't fly to Sark.

14 **Look and match the sentence halves.**

1 I'm happy here because
2 We sometimes play sports but
3 The beaches are clean but
4 There isn't an airport and

a there aren't any cars.
b they're very quiet.
c my family and friends are here.
d there aren't many people to play.

SOUNDS FUN!

15 1:51 **Listen, read and say.**

Popp**y** rides her **b**ike on the **b**each **b**ut her **p**arents are near the **p**yramids on a **b**ig **b**oat a**b**road.

IN THE LOST WORLD OF ATLANTIS

ATLANTIS

1 Yes, those weird guys that took the THD were here. Come on, let's go to the control centre.

We're in Atlantis?

2 What are those guys doing?

I think they're looking for something.

MALL SEA CONTROL CENTRE

3 They were here. They said their names are Zeb and Dot Martin. They wanted to buy a space-time chip, model 3PX40.

3PX40

A what?

4 It's an important chip for a time-travel machine.

There are three in the THD. And I've got a spare 3PX40 in here.

Guys, someone's coming! Quick, hide!

3PX40

5 Where are we going now?

Well, I'm hungry.

MALL

6 And I think Zeb and Dot Martin are hungry, too.

  Act out the story.

Can understand a simple story / Can discuss a story

18 ⭐ What do you know?

19 🎧 1:55 Read. Where are the places in the photos?

Cool places

There are some very interesting cities, towns and villages in the world. Here are some of them. Which do you want to see?

Barcelona, Spain

Look at these beautiful chimneys! They are on the roof of a house in Barcelona. They are by Antoni Gaudí. Gaudí was a famous Spanish architect.

This is a nice place to sit but it is noisy in the summer. It is in a big park and it looks like a snake! Its name is the Serpentine Bench.

Bourton-on-the-Hill and Bourton-on-the-Water, Britain

One of these villages is on a hill and the other is on a river. In Bourton-on-the-Water, there are little bridges over the river. There are a lot of wonderful, old villages in Britain. They are usually quiet but beautiful.

Alice Springs, Australia

Alice Springs is a town in the middle of the desert. A lot of tourists want to visit Alice Springs because the world-famous Uluru, or Ayers Rock, is near the town.

20 Circle.

1 The chimneys by Antoni Gaudí are in (Spain / Britain).

2 The Serpentine Bench is (next to a museum / in a park).

3 Bourton-on-the-Water is (on a river / next to the sea).

4 Alice Springs is (a rock / a town).

MINI PROJECT

21 Find out about an interesting place. Then write.

- **Ideas** – Choose a famous place anywhere in the world.

- **Plan** – Make detailed notes about it.
  Where is it? What's there? Who lives there?
  What can you do there? Is it noisy/quiet/beautiful/hot, etc.?
  Why do you like it?

- **Write** – Use your notes. Write a paragraph about the place.

- **Share** – Tell a classmate about the famous place that you chose.

HOME SCHOOL LINK

22 Write the words.

 1 _____

 2 _____

 3 _____

 4 _____

 5 _____

 6 _____

23  **Listen and choose the right words.**

1:57

1 The supermarket is (near / next to) the park.
2 The library is (behind / next to) the cinema.
3 The swimming pool is (behind / in front of) the shopping centre.
4 The (castle / library) is between the river and the park.
5 (Jim's house / Ann's house) is opposite the shopping centre.

24 Find the sentences and write. Then number.

a to / library / ? / the / go / to / want / you / do
_____

b want / I / to / supermarket / to / go / the
_____

c to / watch / I / film / a / want
_____

1	I want to buy something for dinner.
2	Yes, I do. I want some new books to read!
3	Can I come, too? What time does it start?

25 Ask and answer.

1 Where do you want to go this weekend?
2 What do you want to do this weekend?

I CAN

I can say where places are and give directions.
I can talk about what I want/don't want to do.
I can find out and talk about an interesting place.

Puzzle!

26 Where do you want to go?

1 Read the hints.

Z is the first letter.
G is next to I.
P is between R and S.

A is between B and C.
J is between K and L.
V is between U and X.

D is between E and F.
M is between N and O.
W is the last letter.

2 Write the letters.

A	B	C	D	E	F	G	H	I	J	K	L	M
1	2	3	4	5	6	7	8	9	10	11	12	13
	B		C	E		F	H	I		K		L

N	O	P	Q	R	S	T	U
14	15	16	17	18	19	20	21
N		O	Q	R		S	T

V	W	X	Y	Z
22	23	24	25	26
U		X	Y	

3 Change the numbers to letters.

19	16	20	21	16	7	7	9	4	5
20	13	4	21	8	9	20	2	20	14
4	9	3	2	16	21	21	16	26	8
8	2	20	3	20	18	3	16	9	16
16	18	21	11	19	3	6	11	15	19
16	3	13	5	9	19	9	20	15	7
13	18	5	18	21	3	22	8	9	9
15	25	5	25	3	18	15	16	14	14
2	3	14	11	13	11	5	19	10	10
20	21	3	21	9	16	14	5	19	25
16	3	9	18	19	16	18	21	16	3
7	3	4	21	16	18	25	8	16	13
5	3	18	4	3	6	5	23	13	13
18	5	20	21	3	22	18	3	14	21

4 Find and cross out the place names, i.e. ~~school~~.

27 I want to know more!

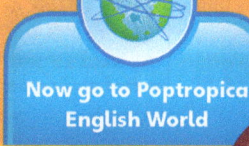

Now go to Poptropica
English World

Wider World 2

Our homes

1  What do you know?

2  Look and say. Guess the three countries. Then listen and check.

1:58

3 Read. Match the texts with the photos.

a

I'm from a small town in Andalucía, Spain. My house is very unusual. It's a cave house. Some people think caves are scary and dark but I think they're great. There are a lot of nice places to visit in my town. A lot of people go to the beautiful beaches at the weekend. It's fun to play volleyball on the sand. The old castles near my house are very interesting, too. My favourite is called Vélez-Blanco. I love my home!

Alba, 11, Spain

b

I live in Hong Kong, a very busy place in Asia. Seven million people live in Hong Kong. It's very noisy here but it's never boring. I live on the fortieth floor of a building in Kowloon. It's got great views. There's a sports centre behind my flat. I go there every day to learn taekwondo. There are a lot of shopping centres, restaurants and museums near my home. The Science Museum is my favourite. I always learn new and interesting things there. I love Hong Kong!

Chiu-Wai, 12, Hong Kong

Can understand texts about where other children live

3

c

I live on an island in Greece called Paros. I live with my family in a beautiful white house in a village. The island is quite small – just 13,000 people live here. There is a harbour near our house. My sister and I like going there and watching the boats. We like sailing too and sometimes we go fishing with our father. My father loves fishing but he's not very good! I love living on an island.

Eleni, 12, Greece

4 **Read again and choose.**

1 Alba lives in a (cave house / beach house) in Spain.
2 She likes going to the (museum / beach) at the weekend.
3 There's a (supermarket / sports centre) behind Chiu-Wai's flat.
4 Chiu-Wai is learning (taekwondo / sailing).
5 Eleni lives (near a river / on an island).
6 Eleni's father is (not good at / good at) fishing.

5  **Ask and answer.**

1 Where do you want to live and why?
2 What do you like about where you live?
3 What don't you like?

YOUR TURN!

Draw your ideal town. Write about it.

This is my ideal town. There's a big cinema...

a cinema
b sports centre
c swimming pool
d museum

1 ⭐ Do you know any dishes from other countries?

2 🎧 2:01 Listen and read. Is Tom happy? Why?

3 🎧 2:02 Listen and say.

1. curry
2. fish and chips
3. soup
4. stew
5. paella
6. spaghetti
7. omelette

4 Do you like the food in Activity 3? Ask and answer.

A: Do you like curry?   **B:** Yes, I love it!

Can identify dishes from other countries

5   **Listen, look and say the correct order.**

a b c d

6 **Match the sentences with the pictures in Activity 5.**

1 Tom paddled very fast.
2 Hannah cooked omelettes.
3 Maria climbed up the climbing wall.
4 They were cold and hungry.

7 **Read and say. Use these words.**

> climbed cooked dropped sailed wanted

1 Yesterday I ❓ dinner for my family.
2 Last week we ❓ new bikes but my mum said, 'No!'
3 A year ago he ❓ Mount Everest.
4 In 2005, she ❓ around the world.
5 Last month they ❓ basketball.

 LOOK!

> I drop**ped** the plate.
>
> He paddle**d** very fast.
>
> Hannah cook**ed** fish and chips.
>
> We love**d** kayaking.

8 **Talk to a friend about last week. Use the words.**

> climbed cooked dropped loved
> was wanted went were

I cooked an omelette!

9 **Listen and say.**

1
pack my bag

2
miss the bus

3
pass a test

4
open a lunchbox

5
remember my juice

6
drop the ball

10  **Listen and sing. Was it a good day or a bad day?**

Chorus:
**It was a bad day, it was really bad
But you smiled at me, now I'm not sad.**

I packed my school bag and walked up the street.
I missed the bus, 'Ow, my tired feet.'
I didn't pass my test, I was late for class.
My friends said, 'Next time, get here fast!'
I opened my lunchbox and said, 'No way!'
I didn't remember my juice today.

Chorus

I went to the park and played with a ball.
I kicked it too hard, it went over a wall.
A boy helped me, he didn't ask why.
We played in the park and we looked at the sky.
I dropped the ball, he said, 'That's OK.'
Now he's my friend and it's a good day.

11  **Read and say. *True* or *false*?**

1 She didn't miss the bus.
2 She was late for class.
3 She remembered her juice.
4 She didn't kick a ball.
5 She dropped the ball.

 **LOOK!**

I **didn't pass** my test.

He **didn't ask** why.

12  **Read and say.**

1 We / not laugh / because we were sad.
2 She / not open / her eyes because it was a scary film.
3 They / play / a second football match because they weren't tired.
4 I / pass / the test because I studied a lot.
5 He / not miss / the bus because he was early.

Lesson 3

Can give reasons for things that somebody did or didn't do using *because*

13 **Read and match the texts with the photos.**

My good day

1 One Saturday last May was a great day for me. I played the guitar in a school concert. I was first onstage and I was scared. I didn't want to play. Then I went onstage and I was OK. I really liked it. Now I want to be a rock star!

Jake, 12

2 My cousin's wedding last year was wonderful. There were a lot of people – about a hundred! The food was great. There was some tasty fish and a tall cake. I didn't want to wear a pink dress but I loved it. Pink is my new favourite colour!

Laura, B

3 Last Friday was a really good day. After school, I went to the park with my friends and we played basketball. Then, a group of girls from another school joined us and we played against them in a competition. We were the winners!

Sandy, 12

14 **Read and say.** *True* or *false?* **Correct the false sentences.**

> False! Jake didn't want to play onstage.

1 Jake wanted to play onstage.
2 Jake played the piano.
3 Laura didn't want to wear a pink dress.
4 There was curry at the wedding.
5 Sandy played basketball in the park last Friday.
6 Sandy and her friends were the winners.

15 **Think of a good day. Tell a friend.**

> Last Saturday was a good day. I went to...

 **SOUNDS FUN!**

16 2:10 **Listen, read and say.**

Donny want**ed** the ball but he pass**ed** it on to Ted.
Ted play**ed** fast but it bounc**ed** off the teacher's head!

ZEB AND DOT ARE AT THE RESTAURANT GASTRONOME.

1

Mm, these dumplings are delicious! Did you make them?

Why yes, I did.

2

It's Dot Martin!

What is she looking for?

3

Eek! It's a rat!

It isn't a rat. It's a meerkat!

4

This is really good.

Um, where did the Martins go?

5

What happened?

I only got one because those kids and that RAT stopped me.

It's not a RAT!

6

Did they just take a food bin?

18   **Act out the story.**

Can understand a simple story / Can discuss a story

19 What do you know?

20 **2:15** Read. What did Ellen do in 2005? What was good/bad?

Amazing Ellen

Ellen MacArthur is a famous British sailor who sailed alone around the world and broke the world record.

1 The Race Around the World

Ellen's race started in November 2004 and finished in February 2005. She broke the world record by thirty-three hours. She became the fastest person to sail around the world alone. When Ellen was at sea, she filmed her journey. We can see her good and bad days on her videos.

2 Bad Times in the Race

It was often dangerous but Ellen was brave. There were storms and big waves. Her food was boring and dry and she was often tired. One very bad day for Ellen was Christmas Day. There was a big storm and it was scary. Ellen phoned her family but she didn't want to talk. She didn't open her Christmas presents.

3 A Good Time in the Race

New Year's Day was good for Ellen. There were no storms. Ellen called her friends and family. She opened her Christmas presents, seven days late and laughed. There were some funny presents. She enjoyed that day.

21 Circle.

1 Ellen started her race in (November / December) 2004.
2 She finished in (2005 / 2006).
3 It was (never / often) dangerous.
4 Ellen (enjoyed / didn't enjoy) Christmas Day 2004.
5 Ellen (phoned / didn't phone) her family on New Year's Day.

MINI PROJECT

22 Choose a famous sportsperson. Write about a special thing they did.

- **Ideas** – Choose a sportsperson who did something very special.
- **Plan** – Make detailed notes about him/her. What did he/she do? When/Where did he/she do it? What was difficult/special about it?
- **Write** – Use your notes. Write a paragraph.
- **Share** – Tell a classmate about your sportsperson's success story.

HOME SCHOOL LINK

23 **Listen and match.**

1 Lenny **2** Jenny and Sam **3** Sally **4** Tom and Rob **5** Laura

24 **Look at Activity 23. Write the verb.**

1 Tom and Rob _____ football because it was very cold.
2 Sally remembered her book when she _____ her bag.
3 Lenny _____ the curry because it was too hot.
4 Laura was late and she _____ the bus.
5 Jenny and Sam are friends because she _____ the ball.

25 **Match.**

1 You make this with eggs.   **a** spaghetti
2 Do this if you don't want to be thirsty.   **b** miss the bus
3 People eat a lot of this in India.   **c** omelette
4 Study hard to do this.   **d** curry
5 Don't do this before school.   **e** remember my juice
6 This is an Italian food.   **f** pass a test

26  **Ask and answer.**

1 What is your favourite food? What food don't you like?
2 Tell me what you did and didn't do this week.
3 Tell me about a very good day in your life.

I CAN

I can talk about things that happened in the past.
I can give reasons for things that did and didn't happen using *because*.
I can find out and talk about a famous sportsperson.

27 **Answer the questions about you. Then interview your friend. Use words from the box. Write your answers.**

HAVE FUN

at the weekend   yesterday

YOU	YOUR FRIEND	YOU	YOUR FRIEND
have a good day?		a place you went to	
Yes, I did.	No, he didn't.	I went to	He went to
do your homework?			
		a person you talked to	
wash the dishes?			
cook the lunch?		something you did	
climb a tree?			
		something you didn't do	
play an instrument?			
watch TV?		something you watched on TV	
pass a test?			
		something you didn't want to do	
help a friend?			

Did you have a good day yesterday?

No, I didn't.

What did you do at the weekend?

I went to the swimming pool.

28   **I want to know more!**

Now go to Poptropica
English World

5 Trips

 What names of tourist attractions do you know?

 2:18 Listen and read. Where was Felipe yesterday?

1. Hi, there! There was an old ticket for Aquafun water park in the tent. Is it yours?

No, it isn't ours. We went to the palace yesterday.

2. Maria, did you go to Aquafun yesterday?

No, I didn't. I went to the museum.

3. Felipe, did you go to Aquafun yesterday?

Yes, I did. It was amazing!

Really?!

3 **2:19** Listen and say.

museum

aquarium

theatre

theme park

palace

water park

botanical gardens

4  Play the game.

A: Maria...
B: ...went to the museum.
A: Yes!

Can identify tourist attractions

5 Listen and choose.

1 Did Maria go to Buckingham Palace?
(Yes, she did. / No, she didn't.)
2 Did Maria go to the aquarium?
(Yes, she did. / No, she didn't.)
3 Did Maria go to the British Museum?
(Yes, she did. / No, she didn't.)
4 Did Maria go to an Indian restaurant?
(Yes, she did. / No, she didn't.)

LOOK!

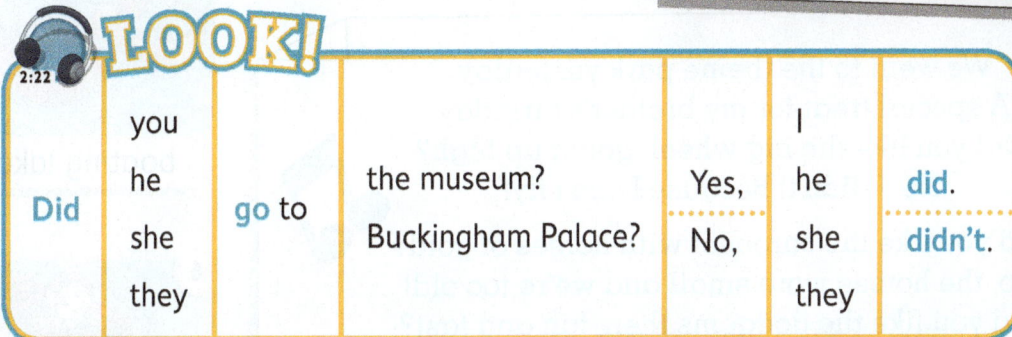

Did	you he she they	go to	the museum? Buckingham Palace?	Yes, No,	I he she they	did. didn't.

 **6** Look and make questions. Ask and answer.

1 ? (✓)   2 ? (✗)

3 ? (✗)   4 ? (✓)

 **7** Think of a place. Ask and answer.

A: Did you go to the beach on Saturday?
B: No, I didn't.
A: Did you go to...

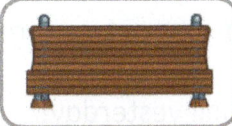

8   **Listen and say.**

1

big wheel

2

dodgems

3

carousel

4

mini-golf

9  **Listen and sing. Where did they go?**

5

boating lake

6

rollercoaster

We went to the theme park yesterday,
A special treat for my brother's birthday.
Did you like the big wheel, going up high?
No, I didn't! Because I can't fly!

Did you like the carousel with horses of gold?
No, the horses were small and we're too old!
Did you like the dodgems then, fun and fast?
No, we didn't! Our car was slow and we were last.

So where did you go? What rides did you like?
Did you like the mini-golf and the boating lake?
No, but we loved the rollercoaster, it was a thrill.
We went on it ten times and now we feel ill!

10  **Look and say the answers.**

LOOK!

Did	you he she we they	like the big wheel?	Yes, No,	I he she we they	did. didn't.

1
Did he play basketball last week?

2

Did they like the carousel?

3
Did we play mini-golf last week?

4
Did she like the boating lake?

11  **Think of a sport and guess. Ask and answer.**

A: Did you play football yesterday?   **B:** No, I didn't.

12 Read. Match the underlined words with the photos a–d.

Newquay is the place to be!

a

b

c

d

Fantastic <u>sandy</u> <u>beaches</u>, great sea and a lot to do!
- Go <u>surfing</u>, sailing or <u>trampolining</u>!
- Visit the aquarium or the water park!
- At New Year, see our amazing <u>fireworks</u>!

There's something for *all* the family!

14th July

Newquay

Hi Gemma,
I'm in Newquay. It's great! Yesterday we went surfing in the sea. The sea was a bit cold. We went trampolining, too. We jumped up and down and got hot again! It didn't rain and we played football on the beach.
The aquarium was good and I really loved the turtles and the fish. We also visited the water park. It was a fantastic holiday and I want to come back next year. Are you enjoying your summer holidays, too?
Love,
Sarah

13 Read and write the answers in your notebook.

1 What activities can you do at Newquay beach?
2 When can you see the fireworks?
3 Did Sarah go in the sea?
4 What was the weather like?
5 Did she enjoy her holiday?

14 Talk to your friend about your last holiday or trip.

A: I went to the beach last summer.
B: Cool! Did you swim in the sea?

SOUNDS FUN!

15  Listen, read and say.

The **theme park** has the **big wheel** but there's **mini-golf** in the **shopping centre**.

1

AT THE THEME PARK

Wow. What happened here?

Ooh! Rides!

I'll tell you what happened! Those weird guys... Grrr!

2

They wanted to go on the ride. They went into a pod.

3

The door closed, then I saw a flash and there was a BANG. And then the pod took off.

BANG

4

But these pods can't fly, can they?

Well, this one certainly flew. It flew right off the ride!

5

Where did it fly?

HOW did it fly?

Hmm, maybe they used the THD for power.

6

Well, it didn't work. Look.

I don't understand. What do those weird guys want?

  Act out the story.

18 **What do you know?**

19 🎧 2:35 **Read. What do the different flags mean?**

BEACH SAFETY iN AUSTRALiA

2

1

Sun safety
- Put on some clothes – always wear a T-shirt or other clothes.
- Put on sun cream – always wear sun cream in the sun.
- Put on a hat – always wear a hat to cover your head in the sun.

Swim safety
- Swim between the red and yellow flags. This water is safe.
- Never swim near a red flag. It means the water is dangerous.
- Always swim near the beach. Don't swim far away.

Surf safety
- Always surf between the surfing signs.
- Always stay with your surfboard.
- Never surf between blue flags.

3

MINI PROJECT

21 **Make a safety poster about a dangerous outdoor activity in your country.**

- **Ideas** – Choose an outdoor activity that can be dangerous.

- **Plan** – Make notes. Think of rules that can make it safe.
  Never... Always... Don't forget to...
  You can... You can't... Wear... Take...

- **Write** – Make a poster like in Activity 19.

- **Share** – Show your poster and tell the class about it.

20 **Answer the questions.**

1 What do you need to wear for sun safety?
a _____
b _____
c _____

2 Where is it dangerous to swim?
_____

3 Where can you never surf?
_____

22 **Circle.**

1 Last week, I went on some cool rides at the (theatre / palace / theme park).

2 First, we went on the (big wheel / mini-golf / carousel) because we like to go up high.

3 Then we went on the (carousel / rollercoaster / dodgems) because it's very fast.

4 My sister is interested in history so she visited the (museum / aquarium / theme park).

23 **Listen and tick (✓). Then write.** 2:36

this morning

1

yesterday morning

2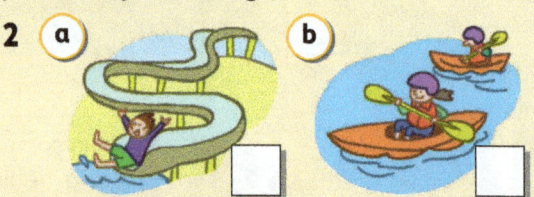

this afternoon

3

yesterday afternoon

4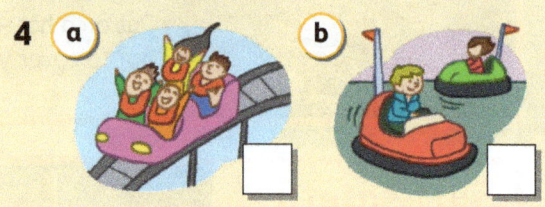

this evening

5

yesterday evening

6

1 What did she do yesterday morning? _____

2 What did she do yesterday afternoon? _____

3 What did she do yesterday evening? _____

24  **Look at Activity 23. Imagine. Then ask and answer.**

1 What did you do yesterday?

2 Did you like the _____?

3 What did you enjoy the most?

I CAN

I can identify tourist attractions and theme park activities.

I can ask and answer questions about trips in the past.

I can make a safety poster.

25 **Draw. Then listen to your friend and draw.**

Design a theme park!

Your theme park

Your friend's theme park

The big wheel is next to the entrance.

26 **I want to know more!**

Now go to Poptropica English World

Wider World 3
Our holidays

1 ⭐ **What do you know?**

2 🎧 2:38 **Look and say. Describe what you see. Then listen and check.**

3 **Read. Match the highlighted words with the photos.**

a

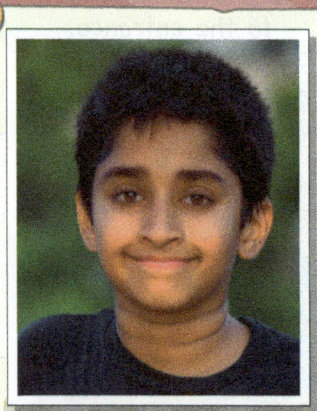

Last year, I went to a city called Agra in India. I visited the Taj Mahal with my family. A man called Emperor Shah Jahan married a princess called Mumtaz Mahal. When she died he was very sad. He built the Taj Mahal for her. Twenty thousand workers and one thousand elephants finished it in 1653. The tombs of Emperor Shah Jahan and his wife are inside the Taj Mahal. I think the Taj Mahal is beautiful!
Samir, 11, India

b

This summer, I went by bus to Cappadocia in Turkey. We stayed in a hotel in front of the Uçhisar Castle. During the day, we visited a city that was inside a mountain. There are houses, restaurants and hotels all inside the mountain. We then went in a hot-air balloon and saw the beautiful Fairy Chimneys.
After that, we visited a famous Turkish bath. I can't wait to visit Cappadocia again next year.
Zeynep, 12, Turkey

Can understand texts about holidays

3

4 **Read again. Answer the questions.**

1 Where is the Taj Mahal?
2 Whose tombs are inside the Taj Mahal?
3 Where was Zeynep's hotel?
4 Name two things you can do in Cappadocia.
5 Who lived in Machu Picchu long ago?
6 What was the Intihuatana Stone?

5  **Ask and answer.**

1 What was your favourite holiday and why?
2 What's a nice place to visit where you live?

c

Last year, I visited a city called Machu Picchu. It's in the Andes Mountains in Peru. Long ago, people called Incas lived in this ancient city. The city was lost in the mountains for hundreds of years. There are ruins of gardens, houses and even a palace. My favourite ruin is called the Intihuatana Stone. It was a big sundial at the top of a big pyramid. There were often special celebrations around the Intihuatana Stone. Machu Picchu is a great place to visit!
Juan, 12, Peru

YOUR TURN!

Ask and answer in your class. Present the results in a graph.

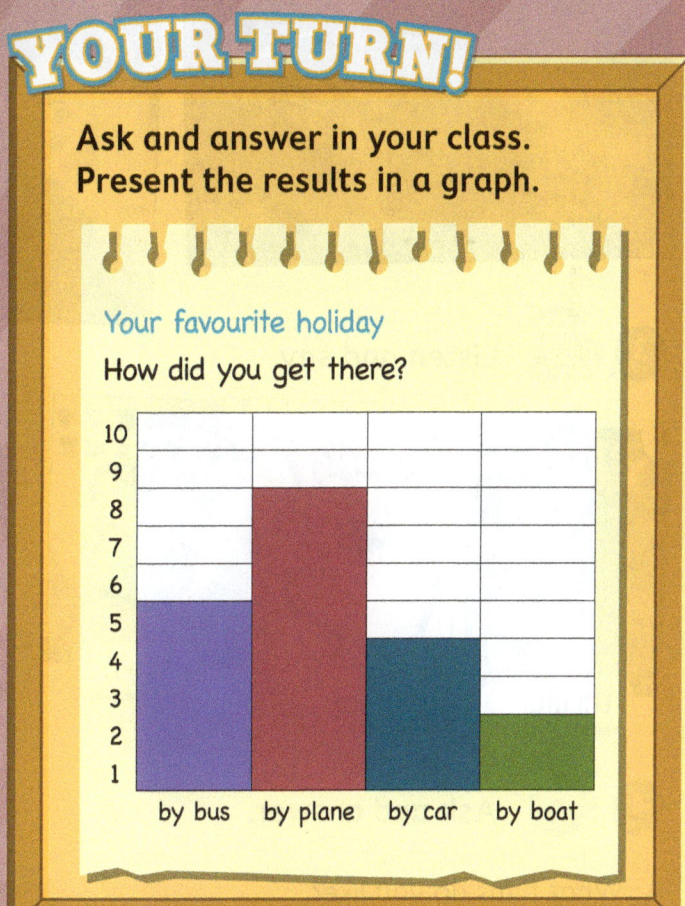

Your favourite holiday
How did you get there?

6 Arts

1 ⭐ What different types of films do you know? Which do you like?

2 2:39 Listen and read. What is *Shadow in the House*?

1 Hi guys! I just saw *Shadow in the House*. It's a scary thriller but I had a great time!

Hi, Maria!

2 There was something in the house. It wrote letters on the window...

3 ...and it made terrible noises.

4 Boo!

Aaah!

Flo, we didn't see you!

5 Sorry!

3  2:40 Listen and say.

1 thriller

2 comedy

3 sci-fi

4 action

5 western

6 romance

7 musical

8 cartoon

4  Ask and answer.

A: What films do you like?
B: I like thrillers and...

Can identify different types of films

5   **Read and say. *True* or *false*?**

1 Maria saw a scary film.
2 Maria didn't have a good time.
3 The shadow didn't write on the window.
4 The shadow made friendly noises.
5 Flo didn't make a scary noise.

LOOK!

have	→	had	→	didn't have
write	→	wrote	→	didn't write
make	→	made	→	didn't make
see	→	saw	→	didn't see

6   **Look and choose. Then listen and check.**

1 The boy (wrote / didn't write) a lot of letters last night.

2 The girl (saw / didn't see) her brother.

3 They (made / didn't make) dinner yesterday.

4 His dad (had / didn't have) a good time at the cinema.

7   **Read and say. Make true sentences for you.**

1 I / write / in my diary last Monday.
2 I / see / a film last week.
3 I / have / a good time last Saturday.
4 I / make / dinner for my family yesterday.
5 I / have / a birthday party last year.

I wrote/didn't write...

8 **2:45** Listen and say. Do you know any other types of music?

9 **2:46** Listen and match with the type of music. Which instruments can you hear?

blues   jazz   pop   rock

a    **b**    **c**    **d**    **e**    **f**

violin   harmonica   saxophone   guitar   drum   piano

10  **2:47 2:48** Listen and sing. How many instruments are in the song?

Chorus:
Did you hear the music last night on the radio?
Did you hear the music last night on the radio?

I didn't feel happy, I was so sad.
But the music was great, it made me feel glad.

Chorus

Yes, I did. Playing funky jazz was a saxophone.
And I loved dancing to it on my own.

Chorus

No, I didn't. Was it pop, was it rock, what was it like?
Country music with guitars and violins, it was all right.

Chorus

Yes, I did. It was the kind of music I choose.
Guitar and harmonica playing the blues.

LOOK!
2:49
Did you **hear** the piano?
Yes, I **did**./No, I **didn't**.

11  **2:50** Listen. Ask and answer.

1   Did you hear a guitar?
2   Did you hear a saxophone?
3   Did you hear a violin?
4   Did you hear a harmonica?
5   Did you hear a piano?

12    Ask and answer.

Did you have a party last month?

have		yesterday
write	**?**	in (January)
make		on (Monday)
see		last (week)

13 **Read. Is the book a thriller, a romance or a comedy?**

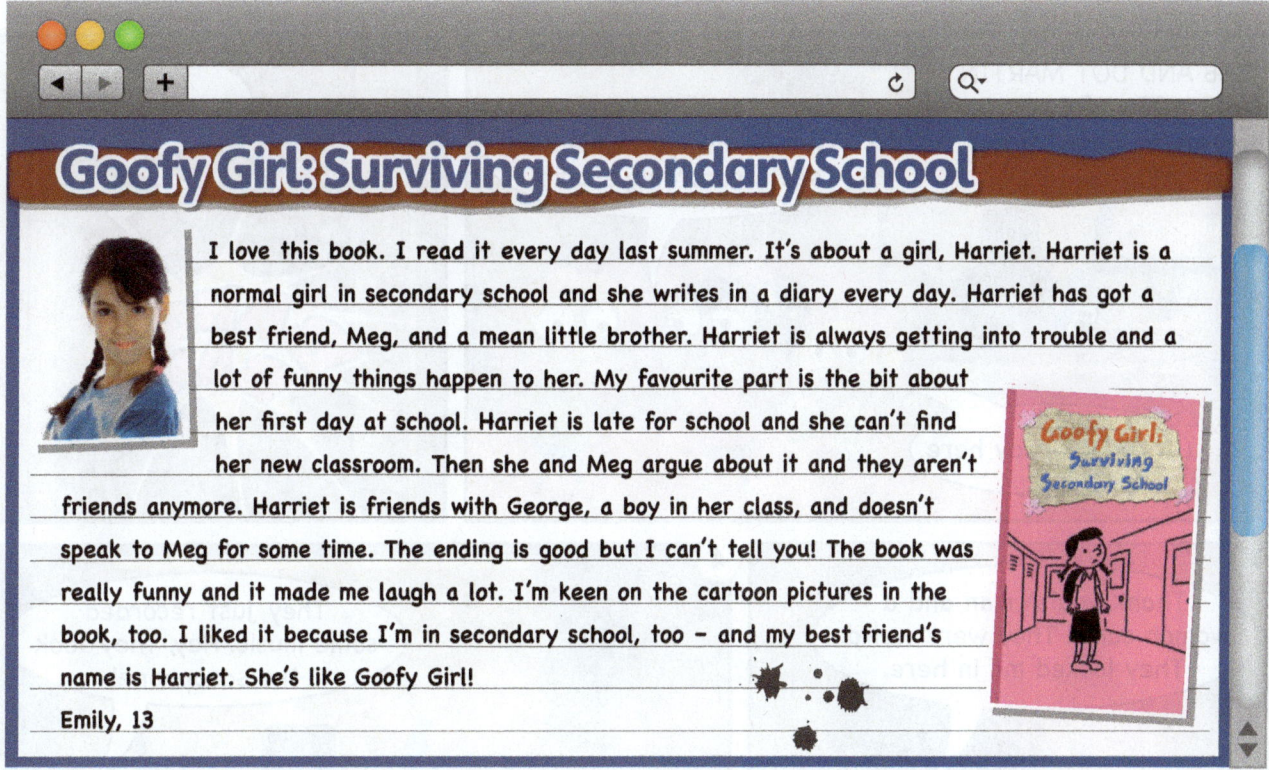

Goofy Girl: Surviving Secondary School

I love this book. I read it every day last summer. It's about a girl, Harriet. Harriet is a normal girl in secondary school and she writes in a diary every day. Harriet has got a best friend, Meg, and a mean little brother. Harriet is always getting into trouble and a lot of funny things happen to her. My favourite part is the bit about her first day at school. Harriet is late for school and she can't find her new classroom. Then she and Meg argue about it and they aren't friends anymore. Harriet is friends with George, a boy in her class, and doesn't speak to Meg for some time. The ending is good but I can't tell you! The book was really funny and it made me laugh a lot. I'm keen on the cartoon pictures in the book, too. I liked it because I'm in secondary school, too – and my best friend's name is Harriet. She's like Goofy Girl!

Emily, 13

14 **Read and choose.**

1 Emily read the book:
   a last week.
   b last summer.
2 The two girls in the book were:
   a Harriet and Meg.
   b Harriet and Evan.
3 The two girls were friends:
   a all the time.
   b most of the time.
4 The book made Emily:
   a laugh a lot.
   b cry a lot.

15  **Talk to a friend about a book. Think about these questions.**

• Is it a comedy/thriller/romance?
• Who are the characters?
• Why do you like it?

SOUNDS FUN!

16 **2:52** **Listen, read and say.**

I saw a small, cold goat in a boat.
I said to him, 'Here, have my yellow coat.'

18 **Act out the story.**

19 **What do you know?**

20  **Read. Do you like the poem?**

Zebra question

by Shel Silverstein

I asked the zebra
Are you black with white stripes?
Or white with black stripes?
And the zebra asked me,
Are you good with bad habits?
Or are you bad with good habits?
Are you noisy with quiet times?
Or are you quiet with noisy times?
Are you happy with some sad days?
Or are you sad with some happy days?
Are you neat with some sloppy ways?
Or are you sloppy with some neat ways?
And on and on and on and on
And on and on he went.
I'll never ask a zebra
About stripes
Again.

21  **Find the opposites of these words in the poem.**

1	good	**2**	neat
3	black	**4**	quiet

22 **Choose three questions from the poem. Ask and answer.**

> Are you good with bad habits?

> Yes, but I haven't got a lot of bad habits.

MINI PROJECT

23 **Find and share a poem you like.**

- **Ideas** – Think about what kind of poems you like and where you can find poems in English.

- **Plan** – Read some English poems and choose your favourite.

- **Practise** – Practise reading your poem aloud. Pay attention to your pronunciation.

- **Share** – Read your poem out loud to the class.

24  Listen, find and say the instrument.

 a

 b

 c

d

e

25  Listen and number.

 a

b

 c

d

e

 f

26 Make questions. Ask and answer.

1   Yes, I went to Paris last summer.
2   No, I didn't play football yesterday.
3   Yes, I saw my English teacher at the park yesterday.
4   No, I didn't go to the theatre last weekend.
5   Yes, I wrote a poem about my family.
6   No, I didn't make a cake today.

Did you go to Paris last summer?

Yes, I went to Paris last summer.

I CAN

I can identify different types of films and musical instruments.
I can talk about things I did or didn't do.
I can find and share a poem I like.

Can assess what I have learnt in Unit 6

27 Answer the questions. Then tell your partner your answers. Your partner has to guess the question.

Guess the Question?

1 Did you come to school on foot or by car today? 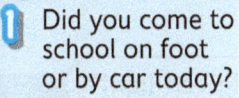 ___	**2** Was the teacher angry with you today? 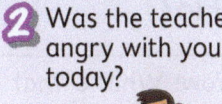 ___	**3** Did you have a good time the last time you went to the theatre?  ___	**4** Did you help your friends today?  ___	**5** Did you eat popcorn the last time you went to the cinema?  ___
6 Did you have a birthday cake on your last birthday?  ___	**7** Did you eat all your lunch yesterday?  ___	**8** What's your favourite band?  ___	**9** Do you like piano music?  ___	**10** What did you watch on TV last night? ___
11 Which do you like most: a comedy, a cartoon or a thriller? ___	**12** Did you say 'Good morning' today? ___	**13** Do you like scary films? ___	**14** How was the weather yesterday? ___	**15** What music do you listen to when you feel sad? ___

Yes, I did. It was a chocolate cake.

Did you have a birthday cake on your last birthday?

28 Look at other units. Say more things that you did and didn't do yesterday/last week/at the weekend/during the holidays.

I went shopping with my friend at the weekend.

During the last holidays, I went to the cinema five times!

29 I want to know more!

Now go to Poptropica English World

1 ⭐ Do you know the names in English of any things in space?

2 🎧 3:01 Listen and read. Can you see Tom and Flo?

1 Felipe, why are you looking at the sky?

Because it's interesting. Look at the stars – they're beautiful.

2 Wow! What's that big red light?

Maybe it's a new star. Where is it?

3 Here. Maybe it's aliens!

4 Let me see! It isn't aliens, it's just a campfire on the hill.

Who is it?

It's Tom and Flo. Come on, let's go!

5

3 🎧 3:02 Listen and say.

a comet

an alien

a spaceship

an astronaut

1

2 a planet

5

4

7

8 the Moon

3 a telescope

6

9 a star

a satellite

4 What can you see in the sky at night? Tell a friend.

I can see some stars...

Can identify things in space

5 **Read and match.**

1 Who is it?
2 Where is it?
3 Why are you looking at the sky?
4 What's that big red light?

a Because it's interesting.
b Here.
c It's Tom and Flo.
d Maybe it's a new star!

6 **Listen and choose.**

3:05

1 Where was Felipe in his dream?

a b c

2 Why was he there?

a b c

3 What did the spaceship look like?

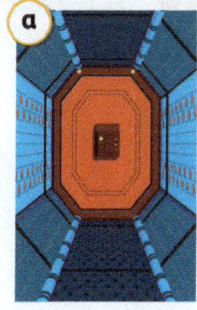  
a b c

4 What did the aliens look like?

a b c

7 **Look at the answers. Make questions.**

When is your birthday?

1 It's on 9th November. **When**
2 She's my mum. **Who**
3 Because it's my birthday. **Why**
4 They're stars. **What**
5 It's next to the swimming pool. **Where**

8 **Ask and answer.**

1 Who is your teacher?
2 Why are you happy/tired?
3 Where is your house?
4 What sports do you like?
5 When is your birthday?

9 3:06 **Listen and say. Then match with the words a–d.**

1	intelligent	**a**	scary
2	amazing	**b**	clever
3	frightening	**c**	very good
4	complicated	**d**	difficult

10  3:07 3:08 **Listen and sing. Does the astronaut like life in space?**

Travel in space is more exciting
Than travel on Earth below.
It's more complicated too and more frightening,
If you really want to know.

The question is – think about it,
Do aliens live out there?
And if they do, are they more intelligent
Than humans everywhere?

I don't know all the answers
But one thing I know is true,
That the world is an amazing place
And it's just right for me and you.

 3:09  **LOOK!**

Travel in space is **more exciting than** travel on Earth.

Are they **more intelligent than** humans?

11 **Make sentences. Do you agree?**

1	English / complicated / Maths
2	A thriller / frightening / a musical
3	Cats / intelligent / dogs
4	Sci-fi films / interesting / romances
5	Snakes / frightening / crocodiles

English is more complicated than Maths.

Can identify and use descriptive words

12 Read Connor's story. What type of story is it?

Connor

The lost spaceship

1 One day in April last year, a spaceship landed in a field. It was only four o'clock in the morning but the noise and the lights woke Jake up. He looked out of his bedroom window.

2 There was a strange object, like a round spaceship, in the field behind his house. A door opened at the bottom of the spaceship and some strange people started walking out into the field.

3 They had large heads and small bodies, and they were green. Jake watched with his mouth open. 'Am I dreaming?' he said. 'Who are those people? Where are they from? What language do they speak?' he wanted to ask them. This was more exciting than any dream.

4 He put on his jeans and a T-shirt, went downstairs and opened the front door. His mum and dad were in bed...

a  b  c  d

13 Look at the pictures. Ask and answer.

A: Picture a?   **B:** Paragraph 3.

SOUNDS FUN!

14 Listen, read and say.
3:10

The **s**mall **st**ars are **sw**imming across the **sk**y.
The **sp**aceship is **sh**aking but I don't know why!

Talk about the pictures. Then listen and read.

ZEB AND DOT BUILT A MACHINE.

1

Look, Dot. We're ready now.

Finally! I can't wait! What do we do now?

2

This will work! Don't worry!

3

They must be here now. They're taking a while.

Wow! Come on, where are you?

4

What is that? A comet?

I don't think so.

Come on! Let's hide over there.

5

Quick!

They're going up!

Here we go. Home time!

6

Are they astronauts?

Hmm, I wonder.

This is the most amazing adventure EVER!

  Act out the story.

Can understand a simple story / Can discuss a story

17 ⭐ What do you know?

18 Read the facts. Number to match the questions with the answers.

Six Space Facts!

1 When did the first men land on the Moon?

2 Where do astronauts sleep in space?

3 Is Saturn closer to the Sun than Jupiter?

4 What colour are stars?

5 Who was the first man in space?

6 How do we know that life was once possible on Mars?

a

In 1969, the astronauts Neil Armstrong and Buzz Aldrin were the first men on the Moon. Armstrong said that it was 'a small step for man but a giant leap for mankind'.

b

In 2011, scientists sent a special robot called the *Curiosity Rover* to Mars. In July 2014, the robot made an amazing discovery. Scientists now believe it is possible that there was life on Mars in the past.

c

They can be different colours. Hot stars are blue, cool stars are red and the Sun is yellow.

d

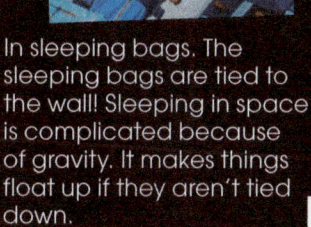

In sleeping bags. The sleeping bags are tied to the wall! Sleeping in space is complicated because of gravity. It makes things float up if they aren't tied down.

e

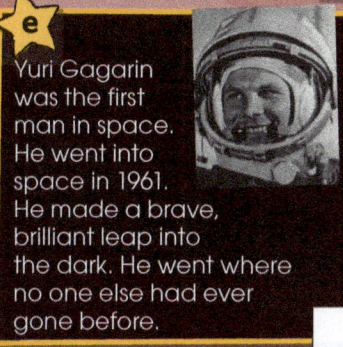

Yuri Gagarin was the first man in space. He went into space in 1961. He made a brave, brilliant leap into the dark. He went where no one else had ever gone before.

f

No, it isn't. It's 1,426 million kilometres from the Sun and Jupiter is 778 million kilometres from the Sun.

MINI PROJECT

SPACE FACTS POSTER

20 Create a poster with fascinating information about space.

- **Ideas** – Look at the space words in Activity 3 on page 58. Choose six that you are interested in.

- **Plan** – Find out some more information about the six space words you chose. Write notes about them.

- **Write** – Look at the model text. Write six questions and one or two facts for each. Draw/Stick some pictures.

- **Share** – Tell your classmate about your space facts poster.

HOME SCHOOL LINK

19  3:15 Listen and check your answers. How many did you know?

21 Look at the pictures and write the words.

1 _____ 2 _____ 3 _____ 4 _____
5 _____ 6 _____ 7 _____ 8 _____

22 🎧 3:16 Write. Then listen and check.

> aliens   astronaut   complicated   the Moon
> planets   frightening   star   telescope

1 The first _____ was Yuri Gagarin.
2 I enjoy looking at the stars in the night sky with my _____.
3 Saturn and Jupiter are _____.
4 Buzz Aldrin and Neil Armstrong were the first men on _____.
5 It is very difficult and _____ to build a spaceship.
6 A lot of people don't want to travel to space. They think it is dangerous and _____!
7 There are a lot of stories about _____ from other planets coming to land on Earth.
8 The closest _____ to the Earth is the Sun.

23 💬 Find and write sentences. Do you agree?

1 Sun / than / more / The / is / Moon / beautiful / the

_____

2 than / more / Jungles / deserts / dangerous / are

_____

3 frightening / more / Aliens / are / crocodiles / than

_____

I CAN

I can identify space words and use words to describe them.
I can ask and answer using *What*, *When*, *Where*, *Who* and *Why*.
I can create a space facts poster.

24 Play. Use space words.

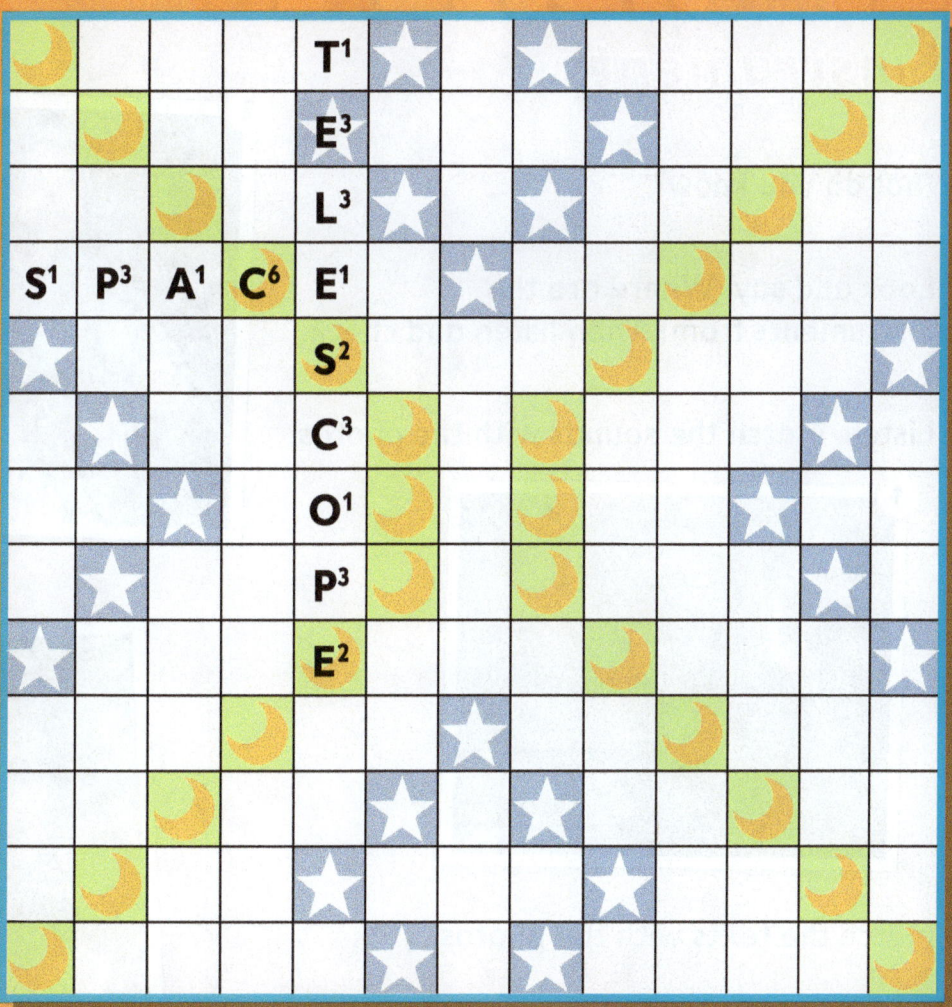

A	B	C	D	E	F	G	H	I	J	K	L	M
Points 1	3	3	4	1	5	3	4	1	8	7	3	5

N	O	P	Q	R	S	T	U	V	W	X	Y	Z
Points 2	1	3	10	2	1	1	1	5	5	10	5	10

Your words	Your points
1	
2	
3	
4	
5	
6	
7	
8	
9	
10	
TOTAL	

How to play

1 Make a word. 2 Write it on the board.
3 Check your points. 4 Write your score.

= **2** x points for the letter

= **3** x points for the letter

25  I want to know more!

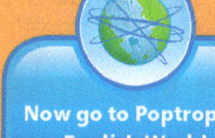
Now go to Poptropica
English World

Wider World 4
World instruments

1  What do you know?

2  3:18 Look and say. Where are the instruments from? Then listen and check.

3 3:19 Listen. Match the sounds with the photos.

4 Read. Match the texts with the photos.

a

I live in Mali, Africa. *Djembe* drums are very famous in my country. People made djembe drums more than 1,500 years ago. These drums are made of hard wood and goat's skin. Sometimes there are lovely pictures of animals or people on them, too. We like listening to the *djembe* drums and dancing. Today, people in Africa play these drums for special celebrations. Famous musicians around the world like playing the *djembe* drums, too.

Moussa, 11, Mali

b

I live in Buenos Aires. People in my country play an instrument called the *bandoneón*. A *bandoneón* player pushes and pulls on the instrument to make beautiful music. It's got square boxes at each end. The boxes are made of wood and have got seventy-one buttons on them. Each button can play two different notes. The *bandoneón* is very difficult to play. It can take ten years to learn. We play the *bandoneón* when people dance the tango. It's great music for dancing!

Marta, 11, Argentina

Can understand texts about musical instruments

3

5 Read again and choose.

1 *Djembe* drums are famous in ❓
   a Argentina.   **b** Mali.   **c** Japan.

2 The boxes on a *bandoneón* are made of:
   a metal.   **b** glass.   **c** wood.

3 Street singers use the ❓ to tell stories.
   a *shamisen*   **b** *djembe* drum   **c** *bandoneón*

4 A *shamisen* has got ❓ strings.
   a six   **b** four   **c** three

5 People made the first *djembe* drum more than ❓ years ago.
   a 40,000   **b** 1,500   **c** 2,000

6 A ❓ has got seventy-one buttons on it.
   a *djembe* drum   **b** *bandoneón*   **c** *shamisen*

6 Ask and answer.

1 What instruments do people play in your country?
2 Can you play an instrument?
3 Which instrument do you want to learn?

c

I'm from Okinawa in Japan. A famous instrument in my country is the *shamisen*. It's like a guitar. It's got a long, thin neck but it's only got three strings. People play it with a short piece of wood. Sometimes, people sing while they play the *shamisen*. Street singers use the *shamisen* to tell stories. People use it in theatre, too. Today, some Japanese rock bands also play the *shamisen*.

Takahiro, 12, Japan

YOUR TURN!

Make a list of some instruments and where they're from.

Djembe drums
– Africa
Shamisen
–

Find out about other instruments from around the world.

1 ⭐ Do you know any ways to help the environment? What are the most important?

2 🎧 3:20 **Listen and read. Why is Flo sad?**

1. It's the last day of camp. I'm sad.
   Come on! Let's clean up!
   I'm going to switch off the lights in the kitchen.

2. Are you going to help?
   Yes, I am. We're going to collect the rubbish.

3. And I'm going to recycle the bottles.

4. Are you going to help, Hannah?
   Well, you're all busy... I'm going to watch!

3 🎧 3:21 **Listen and say.**

1. recycle the paper

2. recycle the bottles

3. collect the rubbish

4. use public transport

5. reuse the bags

6. switch off the lights

4  Look at the words in Activity 3. What does your family do?

5 Read the dialogue again. Who?

1 ❓ and ❓ are going to collect the rubbish.
2 ❓ is going to switch off the lights.
3 ❓ is going to recycle the bottles.
4 ❓ is going to watch.

3:22

LOOK!

I'm going to recycle the bottles.	
He's going to switch off the lights.	
They're going to collect the rubbish.	
Are you going to help?	Yes, I am.
	No, I'm not.

6  Listen and match. Then say.

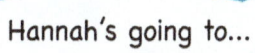3:23

Hannah's going to...

 1    2    3

 a    b     c

7 Look and find these things.

- five things to switch off
- four things to recycle
- five things to clean

 Sam   Kate

8 Imagine you are Sam and Kate. Your parents are going to come home in fifteen minutes. What are you going to do?

I'm going to collect the rubbish.

9   **Listen and say. Then match.**

1	wonderful	a	all places
2	chatter	b	an area of water bigger than a sea
3	beautiful	c	talk
4	everywhere	d	a place bigger than a town
5	city	e	very pretty
6	ocean	f	really good

10  **Listen and sing. What's the singer's answer to the question?**

What's the most beautiful place of all?
Is it the pyramids of Egypt or is it Angel Falls?
I'm going to find out, going to travel everywhere
To see our wonderful world, see it from the air.

I'm going to fly over the blue rivers and seas.
I'm going to hear the monkeys chatter in the trees.
I'm going to see the highest mountains, covered in snow.
I'm going to the busiest cities, full of lights and roads.

So what's the most beautiful place in the world?
I'm not sure I can say, I really don't know.
The mountains, the oceans, the fields of green,
Let's look after this planet and keep it clean,
Keep it clean, keep it clean.
Let's look after this planet and keep it clean.

11 **Look and say. Make sentences.**

1 • tall
  • short

2 • big
  • small

3 • expensive
  • cheap

 **LOOK!**

tall	→ taller than →	the tallest
clean	→ cleaner than →	the cleanest
kind	→ kinder than →	the kindest
important	→ more important than	
	→ the most important	

12 **Make sentences about your class. Tell a friend.**

Marco is the tallest boy in our class.

Can compare things

13 **Read. Ask and answer.**

QUIZ Are you a Green kid?

1 Do you switch off the TV when you're not watching it?
a always **b** sometimes **c** never

2 Where do your fruit and vegetables come from?
a a local market **b** a supermarket **c** your garden

3 It's school tomorrow. Are you going to go:
a by bike? **b** by bus or car? **c** on foot?

4 In the morning, do you have a bath or shower?
a always a bath **b** a bath or a shower **c** only a wash

5 What do you do with rubbish?
a put it in the nearest bin **b** throw it on the floor **c** recycle it

6 At the supermarket, do you:
a always use new bags? **b** sometimes use new bags? **c** always reuse bags

7 When you're in the shower putting on soap, do you turn off the water?
a always **b** never **c** sometimes

8 After a picnic, what do you do with food that isn't finished?
a take it home **b** throw it away **c** give it to the birds

0–14 points You can do better!   **15–24 points** Good, you're a bit green!   **25–30 points** Well done! You're a Green kid!

14  **Listen. What's your score?**

SOUNDS FUN!

15  **Listen, read and say.**

The **ch**eetah mun**ch**es its lun**ch**
on the bea**ch**
And the **sh**y **sh**ark **sh**akes its
shorts in the **sh**ower!

IN THE SPACESHIP

1

Yes, our spaceship broke down - we just want to go home, to Mars.

You're aliens!

2

But why did you take the saxophone? And the food bin?

3

We used the saxophone to send a message to our people and we recycle old food as biofuel.

4

We took the THD to time-travel here. But we need a space-time chip to get home.

I can help... if you give us back the THD.

5

Thank you!

You're welcome!

We'll get home safely now.

6

Well, we must go home now, too.

Yes, sir. Back to Bella's camp, then.

Oh. I'm going to miss you guys!

  Act out the story.

Can understand a simple story / Can discuss a story

18 What do you know?

19 3:37 Read. Then number the photos.

Our Amazing World

a

b

c

d

e

1 The highest waterfall in the world is Angel Falls in Venezuela. It's 979 metres high.

2 Australia is the biggest island and the smallest continent in the world.

3 The Sahara desert in North Africa is the biggest desert in the world. The Atacama desert in Chile, South America, is probably the driest place in the world.

4 The Nile in Africa is the longest river in the world but the Amazon river is a very close second. You can see the Nile in nine countries.

5 Mount Fuji is a very famous volcano in Japan. It's the highest mountain in Japan, too – it's 3,776 metres high.

20 Circle.

1 The highest waterfall in the world is in (Japan / Venezuela).

2 (The Nile / Mount Fuji) is in Japan.

3 The Atacama desert is the (driest / wettest) place in the world.

4 The biggest island in the world is (Japan / Australia).

5 Mount Fuji is (3,776 / 979) metres high.

6 You can see (the Nile / the Amazon river) in nine countries.

MINI PROJECT

21 Write about your amazing country. Create a fact poster.

- **Ideas** – Think about some amazing places.

- **Plan** – Choose five places to write about. Find out some more information about them.

- **Write** – Write one or two facts for each place. Draw/Stick some photos.

- **Share** – Tell your classmate about your places.

HOME SCHOOL LINK

22 Write.

1 _____ the light

2 _____ bottles

3 collect _____

4 use public _____

5 reuse the _____

6 _____ paper

23 Make sentences.

> Tom is taller than Arthur.

1 Tom / tall / Arthur _____

2 Mount Everest / tall / mountain / in the world _____

3 London / big / Paris _____

4 Australia / small / continent / in the world _____

5 The Nile / long / Amazon river _____

6 Dogs / intelligent / cats _____

7 Paris / beautiful / city / in Europe _____

24 What are you going to do:

1 after the lesson?

2 when you get home from school?

3 tomorrow morning?

4 next summer ?

Ask and answer.

> What are you going to do after this lesson?

> I'm going to play football.

> I'm going to have lunch.

> What about you?

I CAN

I can identify ways to help the environment.

I can compare things.

I can create a fact poster about my country.

  25 Play Os and Xs.

I'm going to reuse plastic bags.

  26 Play *Bingo*.

collect rubbish
recycle the bottles
put food in the rubbish bin
recycle paper
reuse plastic bags
recycle plastic bottles
switch off the lights
walk to school
use public transport

  27 Look at other units. Ask more questions with *Are you going to...?*

Are you going to go to the cinema this weekend?

Are you going to pass your test next week?

  28 I want to know more!

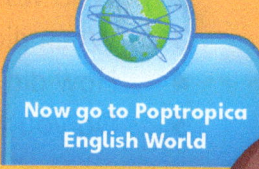
Now go to Poptropica English World

Goodbye

1  **Listen to the summary and number.**

a At Adventure Camp

TODAY'S TASKS
~~PITCH TENTS~~
~~READ COMPASSES~~
LIGHT FIRES
KEEP OUT OF THE RAIN
TAKE DOWN TENTS

b On Future Island

We solved the mystery! They were from Mars

TIME ENGINEER

c Home on Mars

2 **Ask and answer.**

1   What was your favourite scene in the story? Why?
2   Who was your favourite character in the story? Why?
3   When did you start to think that Dot and Zeb were aliens?
4   How did Bella and AL help Matt during the adventure?
5   Do you want to live on Future Island? Why?/Why not?

Can ask and answer questions about the story

3 Which unit are these pictures from?

Unit ____

Unit ____

Unit ____

Unit ____

4 Who said this? Write.

1   'It's there – behind the cinema.'
2   'I was asleep and missed lunch.'
3   '...and it made terrible noises.'
4   'Maybe it's aliens!'

_____ Unit ____
_____ Unit ____
_____ Unit ____
_____ Unit ____

5 Ask and answer.

1   What new things did you learn about nature in this book?
2   Which project was the most complicated?
3   Who was the most brilliant character or person in the book?
4   Which *Have Fun* page was the most fun to do?
5   What was your favourite song in this book? Can you sing it?

6 What was the most important thing your classmates did that helped you learn well together?

_____
_____

Grammar round-up

Unit 1

I love You love He **loves** She **loves** We love They love	play**ing** basketball. sing**ing**. talk**ing**. cook**ing**.

I'm/**I'm not** You**'re**/You **aren't** He**'s**/He **isn't** She**'s**/She **isn't** We**'re**/We **aren't** They**'re**/They **aren't**	**good at**	swim**ming**. danc**ing**. surf**ing**. sing**ing**.

I'm/**I'm not** You**'re**/You **aren't** He**'s**/He **isn't** She**'s**/She **isn't** We**'re**/We **aren't** They**'re**/They **aren't**	sit**ting**. sleep**ing**. cook**ing**. pitch**ing** a tent.

Unit 2

The cat is	**taller than** **longer than** **heavier than** **faster than**	the tortoise.

How tall is the giraffe?	It's 5 metres tall.
How heavy is the hippo?	It's 3,000 kilograms.

opposite

near

Unit 3

I/You **want to**/**don't want to** He/She **wants to**/**doesn't want to** We/They **want to**/**don't want to**	live in a city. watch the sunset. go to the park.

Do you **want to** go to the pool? Yes, I **do**./No, I **don't**.

between

behin

Unit 4

I You He She We They	dance**d**/**didn't dance** at the party. like**d**/**didn't like** the ice cream. dropp**ed**/**didn't drop** the plate. play**ed**/**didn't play** football. walk**ed**/**didn't walk** to the park.

look → look**ed**	like → lik**ed**	drop → drop**ped**
talk → talk**ed**	love → lov**ed**	stop → stop**ped**
pack → pack**ed**	smile → smil**ed**	

Unit 5

Did	I you he/she/we/they	go to the palace? like the museum? dance in the rain?
Yes, I did./No, I didn't.		

	I You He/She We/They	didn't go to the palace. didn't like the weather. didn't watch the film.

Unit 6

have → had → didn't have
hear → heard → didn't hear
make → made → didn't make
see → saw → didn't see
write → wrote → didn't write
say → said → didn't say

Did	you see the concert?	Yes, I did. No, I didn't.
	they hear the piano?	Yes, they did. No, they didn't.

Unit 7

Who is it?
Where is she?
Why are you writing?
What's that red light?
When is your birthday?

One or two syllables	Three syllables or more
scary → scarier than easy → easier than small → smaller than big → bigger than	frightening → more frightening than complicated → more complicated than exciting → more exciting than intelligent → more intelligent than

Unit 8

I'm You're He's/She's We're/They're	going to	recycle the paper. collect the rubbish. switch off the lights. recycle the bottles.
Are you going to recycle the bags? Yes, I am./No, I'm not.		

One or two syllables	Three syllables or more
clean → cleaner than → the cleanest wet → wetter than → the wettest dirty → dirtier than → the dirtiest	important → more important than → the most important intelligent → more intelligent than → the most intelligent expensive → more expensive than → the most expensive

New Year

 1 🎧 3:42 Listen and read. How do children from other countries celebrate New Year?

1

I'm Nahbi. I'm from India. My family celebrates New Year in October. The celebration is called *Diwali*. It lasts for five days! We put special oil lamps in our houses. Sometimes we wear lovely flowers, too.

Hola! I'm Lorena. New Year in Spain is very exciting. On 31st December we go to my granny's house for dinner. She cooks a lot of tasty food for our family. At midnight, everyone eats twelve grapes. Then we watch fireworks in the town square and celebrate with our family and friends.

I'm Li-ying. I live in China. Our New Year celebration is called *Yuan Tan*. We celebrate for nine days. There are big parades with a lot of dancing. Dancers wear big dragon costumes. They dance through the streets and everyone claps!

2

2 Match with the photos.

a dragon costume
b oil lamps
c fireworks

3 Read and answer. *True* or *false*?

1 *Diwali* is the name of the Chinese New Year.
2 *Diwali* lasts for nine days.
3 People in China wear tiger costumes at New Year.
4 People in Spain eat grapes at New Year.
5 Lorena goes to her granny's house at New Year.